THE FEAST THAT ALMOST FLO[PPED]

John 2:1-11 FOR CHIL[DREN]

Written by Carol Greene

Illustrated by Don Kueker

ARCH Books

Copyright © 1973 by Concordia Publishing House, St. Louis, Missouri

Concordia Publishing House Ltd., London, E.C. 1

Manufactured in the United States of America

All Rights Reserved

ISBN 0-570-06076-1

The whole town of Cana was happy and bustling: the day of the wedding had finally arrived! At Barnabas' house the musicians were waiting, and Barnabas watched them, his chest swelled with pride.

For here at *his* house would the wedding take place,
a feast such as never before had been held.
For weeks Mrs. Barnabas cooked and cleaned house
till everything sparkled, and MMMM! how it smelled!

Inside the bride, Rachel, was fixing her hair and adjusting her veil just ever so slightly.

Outside the groom, Daniel, was chewing his beard while butterflies danced and the flowers smiled brightly.

At last the big garden was brimming with guests,
all dancing and singing a wedding-day tune
and gobbling up goodies and gulping down wine
and OOHing and AHing the bride and the groom.

Now Jesus, His mother, and several disciples
were there having fun with the rest of the guests.
"I'm so glad they've come, for they're really quite special!"
said Barnabas proudly, his thumbs on his chest.

"You see, Mrs. B., I'm the best host in Cana. At wedding-feast giving the first prize is mine."

Then up ran a servant, all trembling and panting. "O Barnabas, sir, we've just run out of wine!"

Now this was a serious state of affairs.
To run out of wine would mean total disgrace.
"I boasted too much, and I planned not enough,"
moaned Barnabas, beads of sweat dotting his face.

"Look, Jesus!" cried Mary, who'd heard the whole thing.
"They've run out of wine, and that poor man looks sick.
A miracle would be so easy for You.
Please, Jesus, make Barnabas more wine—and quick!"

Jesus looked at His mother and said very sternly, "My Father's plan must come first, Mother. Not you." Then he turned and saw Rachel and Daniel so happy and knew what His Father would want Him to do.

"Go fill these six jugs with fresh water," said Jesus.
The servants ran quickly to do what He said,

then dipped out a cup and to Barnabas hurried.
(He stood in a corner, still mopping his head.)

He took just a sip, and his face beamed with pleasure. "Why, this is the best wine I've tasted all year!

The groom must have brought it. Now, tell the truth, Daniel.
When did you sneak in and leave the wine here?"

Daniel just stood there and hugged Rachel tighter.
"*I* didn't do it," he said with a grin.
The servants all knew though, and did their
tongues flutter!
" 'Twas Jesus who did it! The wine came from Him!"

And soon all the garden was buzzing with whispers:
"This Jesus *is* God's Son! A good Friend! And mighty!"
They thanked Him and praised Him and then went
on feasting
while butterflies danced and the flowers smiled brightly.

DEAR PARENTS:

Sometimes we forget that most of Jesus' life was as ordinary as the lives of everyone else in His time. He enjoyed the same cool breezes as everyone else, and He took shelter from the same scorching sun. He ate, drank, worked, rested—and had fun. Let the child try to imagine some things Jesus might have done to have fun. Obviously one was going to parties.

At this particular party in Cana, Jesus worked a miracle. He changed water into wine. But, as wonderful as the miracle itself is, what is even more wonderful is the love that lay behind Jesus' action. He saw that the host was about to be embarrassed. To run out of wine would be a dreadful loss of face for a man in that position. Furthermore, the guests would be deprived of their refreshment.

Jesus loved these people. He didn't want them to be unhappy. And he realized that His Father didn't want them to be unhappy either. So, very quietly, He did something about the situation.

At this point the story shows its real meaning for our lives. Jesus loves us too. He doesn't want us to be unhappy. He doesn't change water to wine anymore, but He still works miracles, daily and everywhere, through the actions of those who love Him and one another.

Help the child think of situations in which he can be one of Jesus' miracle workers. No one is too young!

THE EDITOR